Connected  Mathematics

Say It with Symbols

Algebraic Reasoning

Student Edition

Glenda Lappan
James T. Fey
William M. Fitzgerald
Susan N. Friel
Elizabeth Difanis Phillips

PEARSON

Prentice
Hall

Needham, Massachusetts
Upper Saddle River, New Jersey

Connected Mathematics™ was developed at Michigan State University with the support of National Science Foundation Grant No. MDR 9150217.

This project was supported, in part,
by the
National Science Foundation
Opinions expressed are those of the authors
and not necessarily those of the Foundation

The Michigan State University authors and administration have agreed that all MSU royalties arising from this publication will be devoted to purposes supported by the Department of Mathematics and the MSU Mathematics Education Enrichment Fund.

Many of the designations used by manufacturers to distinguish their products are claimed as trademarks. Where those designations appear in this book, and the Publisher was aware of a trademark claim, the designations have been printed in initial caps or all caps.

Photo Acknowledgements: 6 © Mike Valeri/FPG International; 7 © Jeff Greenberg/Peter Arnold, Inc.; 11 © Medford Taylor/Superstock, Inc.; 14 © Mike Greenlar/The Image Works; 17 © Superstock; 24 © Gale Zucker/Stock, Boston; 29 © Cathlyn Melloan/Tony Stone Images; 41 © Elizabeth Crews/The Image Works; 48 © Peter Menzel/Stock, Boston

ISBN 0-13-180828-1

4 5 6 7 8 9 10   07 06 05

The Connected Mathematics Project Staff

Project Directors

James T. Fey
University of Maryland

William M. Fitzgerald
Michigan State University

Susan N. Friel
University of North Carolina at Chapel Hill

Glenda Lappan
Michigan State University

Elizabeth Difanis Phillips
Michigan State University

Project Manager

Kathy Burgis
Michigan State University

Technical Coordinator

Judith Martus Miller
Michigan State University

Curriculum Development Consultants

David Ben-Chaim
Weizmann Institute

Alex Friedlander
Weizmann Institute

Eleanor Geiger
University of Maryland

Jane Miller
University of Maryland

Jane Mitchell
University of North Carolina at Chapel Hill

Anthony D. Rickard
Alma College

Collaborating Teachers/Writers

Mary K. Bouck
Portland, Michigan

Jacqueline Stewart
Okemos, Michigan

Graduate Assistants

Scott J. Baldridge
Michigan State University

Angie S. Eshelman
Michigan State University

M. Faaiz Gierdien
Michigan State University

Jane M. Keiser
Indiana University

Angela S. Krebs
Michigan State University

James M. Larson
Michigan State University

Ronald Preston
Indiana University

Tat Ming Sze
Michigan State University

Sarah Theule-Lubienski
Michigan State University

Jeffrey J. Wanko
Michigan State University

Evaluation Team

Mark Hoover
Michigan State University

Diane V. Lambdin
Indiana University

Sandra K. Wilcox
Michigan State University

Judith S. Zawojewski
National-Louis University

Teacher/Assessment Team

Kathy Booth
Waverly, Michigan

Anita Clark
Marshall, Michigan

Julie Faulkner
Traverse City, Michigan

Theodore Gardella
Bloomfield Hills, Michigan

Yvonne Grant
Portland, Michigan

Linda R. Lobue
Vista, California

Suzanne McGrath
Chula Vista, California

Nancy McIntyre
Troy, Michigan

Mary Beth Schmitt
Traverse City, Michigan

Linda Walker
Tallahassee, Florida

Software Developer

Richard Burgis
East Lansing, Michigan

Development Center Directors

Nicholas Branca
San Diego State University

Dianne Briars
Pittsburgh Public Schools

Frances R. Curcio
New York University

Perry Lanier
Michigan State University

J. Michael Shaughnessy
Portland State University

Charles Vonder Embse
Central Michigan University

Special thanks to the students and teachers at these pilot schools!

Baker Demonstration School
Evanston, Illinois

Bertha Vos Elementary School
Traverse City, Michigan

Blair Elementary School
Traverse City, Michigan

Bloomfield Hills Middle School
Bloomfield Hills, Michigan

Brownell Elementary School
Flint, Michigan

Catlin Gabel School
Portland, Oregon

Cherry Knoll Elementary School
Traverse City, Michigan

Cobb Middle School
Tallahassee, Florida

Courtade Elementary School
Traverse City, Michigan

Duke School for Children
Durham, North Carolina

DeVeaux Junior High School
Toledo, Ohio

East Junior High School
Traverse City, Michigan

Eastern Elementary School
Traverse City, Michigan

Eastlake Elementary School
Chula Vista, California

Eastwood Elementary School
Sturgis, Michigan

Elizabeth City Middle School
Elizabeth City, North Carolina

Franklinton Elementary School
Franklinton, North Carolina

Frick International Studies Academy
Pittsburgh, Pennsylvania

Gundry Elementary School
Flint, Michigan

Hawkins Elementary School
Toledo, Ohio

Hilltop Middle School
Chula Vista, California

Holmes Middle School
Flint, Michigan

Interlochen Elementary School
Traverse City, Michigan

Los Altos Elementary School
San Diego, California

Louis Armstrong Middle School
East Elmhurst, New York

McTigue Junior High School
Toledo, Ohio

National City Middle School
National City, California

Norris Elementary School
Traverse City, Michigan

Northeast Middle School
Minneapolis, Minnesota

Oak Park Elementary School
Traverse City, Michigan

Old Mission Elementary School
Traverse City, Michigan

Old Orchard Elementary School
Toledo, Ohio

Portland Middle School
Portland, Michigan

Reizenstein Middle School
Pittsburgh, Pennsylvania

Sabin Elementary School
Traverse City, Michigan

Shepherd Middle School
Shepherd, Michigan

Sturgis Middle School
Sturgis, Michigan

Terrell Lane Middle School
Louisburg, North Carolina

Tierra del Sol Middle School
Lakeside, California

Traverse Heights Elementary School
Traverse City, Michigan

University Preparatory Academy
Seattle, Washington

Washington Middle School
Vista, California

Waverly East Intermediate School
Lansing, Michigan

Waverly Middle School
Lansing, Michigan

West Junior High School
Traverse City, Michigan

Willow Hill Elementary School
Traverse City, Michigan

Contents

Say It with Symbols

Christopher says the formula for the perimeter of a rectangle with length L and width W is $P = 2(L + W)$. Vanessa claims the formula is $P = 2L + 2W$. Is it possible that both students are correct?

The height of a ball t seconds after it is thrown is $h = ^-16t^2 + 48t$. How would you use a graphing calculator to estimate the height of the ball after 2 seconds? How would you estimate this height without using a calculator?

Jeff wrote $C = 150 + 5(2N + 10)$ to describe the cost for N students to go on a class trip. How would you use this equation to find the cost for 25 students? How would you write an equation for the average cost per student?

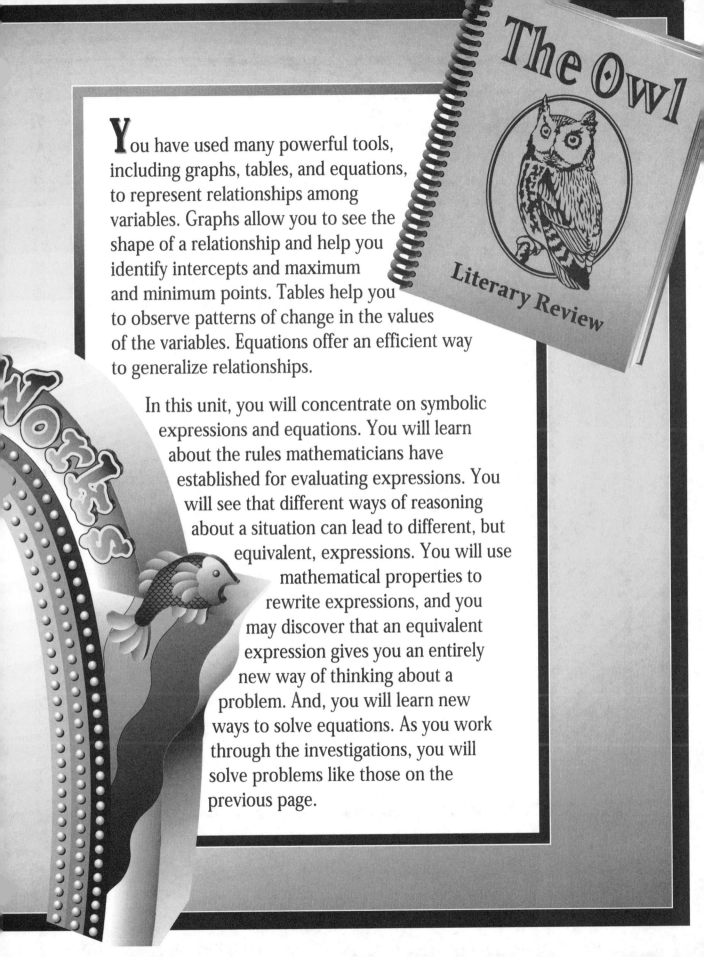

You have used many powerful tools, including graphs, tables, and equations, to represent relationships among variables. Graphs allow you to see the shape of a relationship and help you identify intercepts and maximum and minimum points. Tables help you to observe patterns of change in the values of the variables. Equations offer an efficient way to generalize relationships.

In this unit, you will concentrate on symbolic expressions and equations. You will learn about the rules mathematicians have established for evaluating expressions. You will see that different ways of reasoning about a situation can lead to different, but equivalent, expressions. You will use mathematical properties to rewrite expressions, and you may discover that an equivalent expression gives you an entirely new way of thinking about a problem. And, you will learn new ways to solve equations. As you work through the investigations, you will solve problems like those on the previous page.

The Owl

Literary Review

Mathematical Highlights

In *Say It With Symbols* you will extend your ability to use symbolic expressions to describe and reason about relations between variables. The unit should help you to

- Use *order of operations* rules to write and evaluate algebraic expressions and equations that model quantitative patterns and relationships;

- Interpret given symbolic expressions to discover the relations between variables that are implied by those expressions;

- Understand and apply properties of numbers and operations to write algebraic expressions and equations in equivalent forms; and

- Solve linear and quadratic equations by symbolic reasoning.

As you work on the problems of this unit, make it a habit to ask questions about problem situations that involve symbolic expressions and equations: *What symbolic expression or equation correctly expresses the sequence of calculations required by given conditions? Is there a way that a given expression or equation can be written in equivalent form to provide new information about a relationship? What operations would transform a given equation into an equivalent form from which the solution will be clear?*

Order of Operations

Equations are an efficient way to communicate information about relationships among variables. To help us communicate clearly, mathematicians have established rules for writing and interpreting algebraic expressions. In this investigation, you will explore these rules.

Think about this!

The rugby club wants to order new jerseys. The jersey manufacturer tells the club members that they can figure out the total cost by using the equation

$$C = 100 + 15N$$

where C is the cost in dollars and N is the number of jerseys ordered. The team wants 20 jerseys. Pedro and David both calculate the amount the club will owe.

Pedro's calculation	David's calculation
$C = 100 + 15 \times 20$	$C = 100 + 15 \times 20$
$= 100 + 300$	$= 115 \times 20$
$= 400$	$= 2300$

Who did the calculation correctly? What mistake did the other boy make?

1.1 Adding and Multiplying

The Water Works amusement park features exciting water rides and slides. The park discounts admission prices for large groups. Group prices are determined by using the equation $p = 100 + 10a + 8c$, where p is the price in dollars, a is the number of adults, and c is the number of children.

As part of an advertising brochure, the Water Works marketing manager wants to include a table showing admission prices for groups with certain numbers of adults and children.

Group Admission Prices

Number of children

		20	40	60	80	100
Number of adults	10					
	20					
	30					
	40					

A. Copy and complete the table to show admission prices for groups with various numbers of adults and children. Do your calculations without using a calculator.

B. Look for patterns in the rows and columns of the table. Describe each pattern you find, and tell which part of the equation creates the pattern.

C. In the equation $p = 100 + 10a + 8c$, what do the numbers 100, 10, and 8 tell you about calculating the group price?

D. What mathematical operations do you need to perform to calculate the group price for a particular number of adults and children? In what order must you perform the operations?

Problem 1.1 Follow-Up

The Water Works business manager used data collected over the past several years to write equations that help him make predictions about the daily operations of the park.

1. The daily profit in dollars, P, from the park concession stands depends on the number of visitors, V. The business manager wrote the equation $P = 2.50V - 500$ to model this relationship.

    a. If 300 people visit the park, about how much concession profit will be made? Do your calculations without using a calculator.

    b. If 600 people visit the park, about how much concession profit will be made? Do your calculations without using a calculator.

    c. What mathematical operations did you perform to calculate your answers in parts a and b? In what order did you perform the operations?

    d. Check your answer from part a by entering $2.5 \times 300 - 500$ on a graphing calculator and pressing $\boxed{\text{ENTER}}$. Check your answer for part b by entering $2.5 \times 600 - 500$ and pressing $\boxed{\text{ENTER}}$. Do the results agree with the results you found by doing the calculations by hand?

2. The manager uses the equation $V = 600 - 500R$ to predict the number of visitors based on the probability of rain, R.

    a. If the probability of rain is 25%, about how many people will visit the park? Do your calculations without using a calculator.

    b. If the probability of rain is 75%, about how many people will visit the park? Do your calculations without using a calculator.

    c. What mathematical operations did you perform to calculate your answers in parts a and b? In what order did you perform the operations?

    d. Use a graphing calculator to check your answers from parts a and b. Do the results agree with the results you found by doing the calculations by hand?

3. Use the equations from questions 1 and 2 to answer these questions.

    a. If the probability of rain is 50%, about how much profit will be made from the concession stands?

    b. If the probability of rain is 10%, about how much profit will be made from the concession stands?

    c. What mathematical operations did you perform to calculate your answers in parts a and b? In what order did you perform the operations?

4. You can combine the equations from questions 1 and 2 into a single equation. Since $V = 600 - 500R$, you can substitute the expression $600 - 500R$ for V in the equation $P = 2.50V - 500$. This gives the equation $P = 2.50(600 - 500R) - 500$, which tells you the expected concession profit in terms of the probability of rain. The parentheses indicate that you should evaluate $600 - 500R$ *before* multiplying by 2.50.

    a. Use this equation to find the expected concession profit if the probability of rain is 50% and if the probability of rain is 10%. Check both results with your calculator.

    b. How do your answers compare with the results you found in parts a and b of question 3?

5. The equations used by the Water Works business manager involve addition, subtraction, and multiplication. When you evaluate expressions with these operations, in what order should you perform the operations? For example, what steps would you follow to evaluate $40 - 5x + 7y$ when $x = 3$ and $y = 5$?

1.2 Dividing

As with division of numbers, division of algebraic expressions is often shown as a fraction. In the last problem, you saw that the daily concession profit at Water Works can be predicted by the equation $P = 2.50V - 500$. The business manager used this profit equation to derive the following equation for the average daily concession profit per visitor:

$$A = \frac{2.50V - 500}{V}$$

Problem 1.2

A. 1. If 300 people visit the park, about how much concession profit will be made?

2. About how much concession profit will be made per visitor?

B. Copy and complete the table below to show the average per-visitor concession profit for various numbers of visitors. Do your calculations without using your calculator.

Visitors	100	200	300	400	500	600	700	800
Average profit								

C. Find the average per-visitor concession profit for 250, 350, and 425 visitors.

D. What mathematical operations do you need to perform to calculate the average per-visitor profit for a given number of visitors? In what order must you perform the operations?

E. The Water Works business manager claims that the average concession profit per visitor can also be calculated with either of these equations:

$$A = \frac{1}{V}(2.50V - 500) \qquad A = (2.50V - 500) \div V$$

Do you agree? Explain.

▪ Problem 1.2 Follow-Up

1. a. Use the example of calculating the average per-visitor concession profit as a guide to help you evaluate $\frac{100 + 3x}{x}$ when $x = 25$.

b. Check your answer by entering an expression into your graphing calculator and pressing $\boxed{\text{ENTER}}$. What expression did you enter?

2. a. Use the example of calculating the average per-visitor concession profit as a guide to help you evaluate $\frac{3x}{4x + 3}$ when $x = 10$.

b. Check your answer by entering an expression into your graphing calculator and pressing $\boxed{\text{ENTER}}$. What expression did you enter?

3. When evaluating an expression that is in fraction form, in what order should you perform the operations?

1.3 Working with Exponents

The president of Water Works wants a large arch built at the entrance to the park. He gave the architect the sketch and equation below. The equation gives the height, y, of the arch above a point x feet from one of the bases of the arch. This means that if you are standing under the arch x feet from one base, the point of the arch directly over your head will be $5x - 0.1x^2$ feet above the ground.

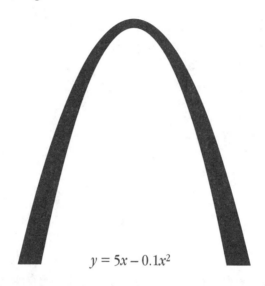

$$y = 5x - 0.1x^2$$

Problem 1.3

A. Use the equation to find the height of the arch at these distances from the left base. Do your calculations without using a calculator.

1. 10 feet

2. 30 feet

3. 50 feet

B. What operations did you perform to calculate your answers for part A? In what order did you perform these operations?

C. Check your answers for part A by using a graphing calculator to help you make a table.

D. 1. The expression $5x - 0.1x^2$ is equivalent to the expression $0.1x(50 - x)$. Use this second expression to calculate the heights for the x values given in part A.

2. In what order did you perform the operations?

■ Problem 1.3 Follow-Up

When a giant roller coaster was built at Water Works, attendance began to increase. The business manager wrote the equation $V = 1000(1.2^m)$ to estimate the daily number of visitors m months after the roller-coaster ride opened.

1. a. Estimate the number of visitors 1 month after the roller-coaster ride opened.

   b. Estimate the number of visitors 5 months after the roller-coaster ride opened.

   c. Estimate the number of visitors 12 months after the roller-coaster ride opened.

2. What operations did you perform to find your answers in question 1? In what order did you perform the operations?

3. Check your answer to part c of question 1 by entering an expression into your calculator and pressing ENTER. What expression did you enter?

Did you know?

Americans have been splashing at water-slide parks for more than 100 years! The first water park was opened in 1894 in Chicago's South Side by Captain Paul Boynton. The popular and successful "Captain Boynton's Water Chutes" was the first modernized amusement park in the world. The parked served as a model for amusement parks built during the recreation boom of the early 1900s.

As you work on these ACE questions, use your calculator whenever you need it.

Applications

In 1–5, evaluate the expression for the given x value, and describe the order in which you performed the operations.

1. $3x + 15$ when $x = 12$

2. $25 + 8x$ when $x = 2$

3. $10x - 12$ when $x = 4$

4. $^-3x + 10$ when $x = 7$

5. $40 - 5x$ when $x = 6$

In 6–9, evaluate the expression for the given x value, and describe the order in which you performed the operations.

6. $5x^2$ when $x = 4$

7. $5x^2$ when $x = {}^-3$

8. $^-3x^2$ when $x = 4$

9. $^-3x^2$ when $x = {}^-4$

In 10–17, evaluate the expression for the given x value, and describe the order in which you performed the operations.

10. $4x^2 + 3x$ when $x = 7$

11. $4x^2 + 3x$ when $x = {}^-7$

12. $4x^2 - 3x$ when $x = 7$

13. $4x^2 - 3x$ when $x = {}^-7$

14. $4x^2 + 3x + 5$ when $x = 2$

15. $4x^2 + 3x - 5$ when $x = 2$

16. $4x^2 - 3x - 5$ when $x = {}^-3$

17. $^-4x^2 - 3x - 5$ when $x = {}^-3$

In 18–22, evaluate the expression for the given x value, and describe the order in which you performed the operations.

18. $7(x + 8)$ when $x = {}^-3$

19. $7(5x + 8)$ when $x = 3$

20. $7(8 - 5x)$ when $x = 3$

21. $(8 - 5x)(3x + 2)$ when $x = 4$

22. $(x - 5)(x + 2)$ when $x = 10$

In 23–27, evaluate the expression for the given x value, and describe the order in which you performed the operations.

23. $\frac{36}{2x}$ when $x = 6$

24. $\frac{3x + 2}{5}$ when $x = 11$

25. $\frac{72}{2x + 1}$ when $x = 4$

26. $\frac{50x + 10}{x}$ when $x = 2$

27. $\frac{8 + 3x}{x + 1}$ when $x = 4$

28. **a.** Find the value of $2 + 3x \div 2$ when $x = 4$.

b. Write an expression that is equivalent to $2 + 3x \div 2$ and that includes a fraction.

c. Evaluate the expression you wrote in part b for $x = 4$. How does your result compare to the result you found in part a?

Connections

In 29 and 30, use this information: The ski club is planning a trip for winter break. They wrote the equation $C = 200 + 10N$ to estimate the cost in dollars of the trip if N students attend.

29. Duncan and Gish both used the equation to estimate the cost for 50 students. Duncan said the cost would be $10,500, and Gish said it would be $700.

a. Determine which estimate is correct. Show the calculations needed to find the estimate.

b. How do you think Duncan and Gish found such different estimates if they both used the same equation?

30. **a.** Write an equation for the cost per student, S, if N students go on the trip.

b. What will be the cost per student if 20 students go on the trip?

c. What will be the cost per student if 40 students go on the trip?

In 31–33, you will explore some relationships involved in the operation of Water Works.

31. The concession profit, in dollars, for V visitors can be estimated by the equation $P = 2.50V - 500$.

    a. Make a table of data for five V values.

    b. Graph the equation.

    c. Identify the slope and the y-intercept of the graph. Explain what each of these values tells you about the relationship between the variables.

32. The number of visitors can be estimated from the probability of rain, R, by using the equation $V = 600 - 500R$.

    a. Make a table of data for five R values.

    b. Graph the equation.

    c. Identify the slope and the y-intercept of the graph. Explain what each of these values tells you about the relationship between the variables.

33. The daily increase in the employee-bonus fund, in dollars, can be estimated from the number of visitors by using the equation $B = 100 + 0.50V$.

    a. Make a table of data for five V values.

    b. Graph the equation.

    c. Identify the slope and the y-intercept of the graph. Explain what each of these values tells you about the relationship between the variables.

In 34–39, you will practice evaluating familiar geometric formulas. As you evaluate each formula, think carefully about the order of operations.

34. The formula for the area of a circle with radius r is $A = \pi r^2$. Find the area of a circle with a radius of 4 centimeters.

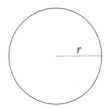

35. The formula for the surface area of a cube with edges of length e is $A = 6e^2$. Find the surface area of a cube with edges of length 5 centimeters.

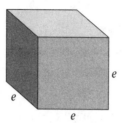

36. The formula for the volume of a cone with radius r and height h is $V = \frac{1}{3}\pi r^2 h$. Find the volume of a cone with a radius of 7 centimeters and a height of 10 centimeters.

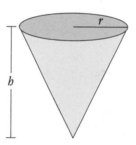

37. The formula for the surface area of a cylinder with radius r and height h is $A = 2\pi r^2 + 2\pi rh$. The $2\pi r^2$ part represents the area of the circular top and bottom, and the $2\pi rh$ part represents the "side" that can be unrolled to form a rectangle. Find the surface area of a cylinder with a radius of 3 centimeters and a height of 8 centimeters.

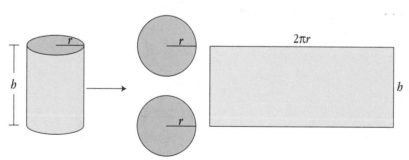

38. The formula for the area of a circle with radius r is $A = \pi r^2$. Tina, Hyung, and Jamal used this formula to estimate the area of a pizza with a diameter of 9 inches. They each found a different area. In a–c, decide whether the student's estimate is reasonable. If the estimate is not reasonable, figure out what mistake the student might have made in his or her calculation.

a. Tina estimated the area to be about 254 square inches.

b. Hyung estimated the area to be about 200 square inches.

c. Jamal estimated the area to be about 64 square inches.

39. The formula for the surface area of a sphere with radius r is $A = 4\pi r^2$.

a. Find the surface area of a globe with radius 1 foot.

b. The radius of Earth is about 4000 miles. Find the surface area of Earth.

c. The radius of the sun is about 430,000 miles. Find the surface area of the sun.

d. What is the ratio of Earth's radius to the sun's radius?

e. What is the ratio of Earth's surface area to the sun's surface area?

f. How does your ratio from part d compare to your ratio from part e?

40. A bacterium colony begins with 5000 bacteria. The population doubles every hour. This pattern of exponential growth can be modeled by the equation $b = 5000(2^t)$, where b is the number of bacteria and t is the number of hours.

a. What is the population of the colony after 3 hours? After 5 hours?

b. What mathematical operations did you perform to calculate your answers in part a? In what order did you perform these operations?

41. The equation $d = {}^-16t^2 + 16t + 6.5$ represents the distance in feet from the ground to the top of a basketball player's head t seconds after the player jumps.

   a. Find the distance to the top of the player's head after 0.1 second.

   b. Find the distance to the top of the player's head after 0.3 second.

   c. Find the distance to the top of the player's head after 1 second.

   d. What mathematical operations did you perform to calculate your answers in parts a–c? In what order did you perform these operations?

Extensions

42. The equation $y = 0.1x^2 - 2x + 25$ describes the height of a suspension cable above the bridge it supports as a function of the distance, x, from one end of the bridge. All measurements are in feet. Several students used this equation to estimate the height for different x values.

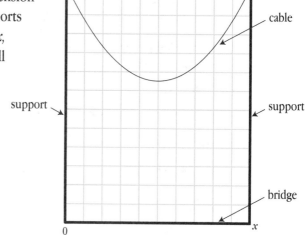

   a. For $x = 10$, Santha calculated a height of 6 feet, and Julio calculated a height of 15 feet. Which student is correct? What error do you think the other student made?

   b. For $x = 20$, Joyce calculated a height of $^-11$ feet, and Donny calculated a height of 25 feet. Which student is correct? What error do you think the other student made?

Mathematical Reflections

In this investigation, you evaluated algebraic expressions for given values of the variables. As you worked, you explored the rules for order of operations. These questions will help you summarize what you have learned:

1 **a.** When an expression involves addition, subtraction, and multiplication, in what order should you perform the operations?

b. Illustrate your answer to part a by writing an appropriate expression and evaluating it for specific values of the variables.

2 **a.** When an expression involves division and other operations such as addition, subtraction, and multiplication, in what order should you perform the operations?

b. Illustrate your answer to part a by writing an appropriate expression and evaluating it for specific values of the variables.

3 **a.** When an expression involves exponents and other operations such as addition, subtraction, and multiplication, in what order should you perform the operations?

b. Illustrate your answer to part a by writing an appropriate expression and evaluating it for specific values of the variables.

Think about your answers to these questions, discuss your ideas with other students and your teacher, and then write a summary of your findings in your journal.

Equivalent Expressions

Throughout your work in mathematics this year, you have
written symbolic expressions and equations to represent
situations involving variables. Because there is usually
more than one way to think about a situation, there is
often more than one way to express the situation in
symbols. For example, consider the perimeter of a rectangle
with length L and width W.

Think about this!

Jim says the perimeter of the rectangle above is $2(L + W)$. Lilia says the
perimeter is $2L + 2W$. How could you convince the students that their
expressions are equivalent?

Since $2(L + W)$ and $2L + 2W$ represent the same quantity, they are **equivalent
expressions**. In this investigation, you will look at situations that can be described with
several different, but equivalent, expressions, and you will see how each expression
represents a unique way of interpreting a situation. You will also learn some methods
for showing that two expressions are equivalent.

2.1 Tiling Pools

Hot tubs and in-ground swimming pools are
sometimes surrounded by borders of tiles. This
drawing shows a square hot tub with sides of length
5 feet surrounded by square border tiles. The border
tiles measure 1 foot on each side. A total of 24 tiles
are needed for the border.

Problem 2.1

In this problem, you will explore this question: If a square pool has sides of length s feet, how many tiles are needed to form the border?

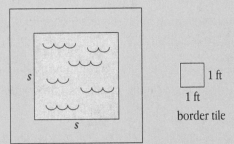

1 ft
1 ft
border tile

A. Make sketches on grid paper to help you figure out how many tiles are needed for the borders of square pools with sides of length 1, 2, 3, 4, 6, and 10 feet. Record your results in a table.

B. Write an equation for the number of tiles, N, needed to form a border for a square pool with sides of length s feet.

C. Try to write at least one more equation for the number of tiles needed for the border of the pool. How could you convince someone that your expressions for the number of tiles are equivalent?

Problem 2.1 Follow-Up

1. Make a table and a graph for each equation you wrote in part a of Problem 2.1. Do the table and the graph indicate that the equations are equivalent? Explain.

2. Is the relationship between the side length of the pool and the number of tiles linear, quadratic, exponential, or none of these? Explain your reasoning.

3. **a.** Write an equation for the area of the pool, A, in terms of the side length, s.
   b. Is the equation you wrote linear, quadratic, exponential, or none of these? Explain.

4. **a.** Write an equation for the combined area of the pool and its border, C, in terms of the side length, s.
   b. Is the equation you wrote linear, quadratic, exponential, or none of these? Explain.

2.2 Thinking in Different Ways

You and your classmates probably found more than one way to express the number of tiles needed for the border of a square pool. Now you will explore how different ways of thinking about this problem lead to different expressions.

Problem 2.2

Takashi thought of the pool's border as being composed of four 1-by-s rectangles, each made from s tiles, and four corner squares, each made from one tile. He wrote the expression $4s + 4$ to represent the total number of border tiles.

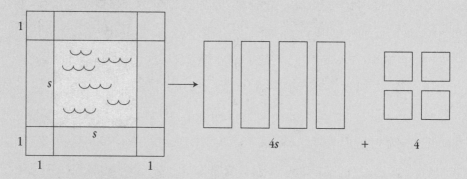

A. Stella wrote the expression $4(s + 1)$ to represent the number of border tiles. Draw a picture that illustrates how Stella might have been thinking about the border of the pool.

B. Jeri wrote the expression $s + s + s + s + 4$ to represent the number of border tiles. Draw a picture that illustrates how Jeri might have been thinking about the border of the pool.

C. Sal wrote the expression $2s + 2(s + 2)$ to represent the number of border tiles. Draw a picture that illustrates how Sal might have been thinking about the border of the pool.

D. Jackie wrote the expression $4(s + 2) - 4$ to represent the number of border tiles. Draw a picture that illustrates how Jackie might have been thinking about the border of the pool.

E. Explain why each expression in parts A–D is equivalent to Takashi's expression.

Problem 2.2 Follow-Up

1. Evaluate each of the five expressions given in the problem for $s = 10$. Can you conclude from your results that all the expressions are equivalent? Explain your reasoning.

2. Make a table and a graph for each of the five expressions. Do the tables and the graphs indicate that the expressions are equivalent? Explain.

2.3 Diving In

Swimming pools are sometimes divided into sections that are used for different purposes. For example, a pool may have a section for lap swimming and a section for diving, or a section for experienced swimmers and a section for small children.

In this problem, you will investigate ways to express the surface area of the water in several divided pools. The problem illustrates an important and useful mathematical property that you will use throughout the remainder of this unit.

Problem 2.3

Below are four designs for pools with swimming and diving sections. For each design, show two methods for calculating the total surface area of the water. Then tell which method is more efficient. That is, tell which method requires fewer mathematical operations.

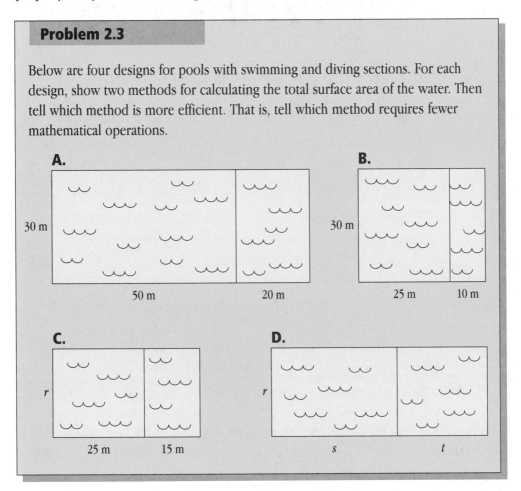

■ Problem 2.3 Follow-Up

As you worked on Problem 2.3, you found two equivalent expressions for the surface area of the water in each pool. For example, to find the surface area of the pool in part A, you might have multiplied the length of the entire pool by its width to get $30(50 + 20)$, and you might have added the areas of the two sections to get $30(50) + 30(20)$. The expressions $30(50 + 20)$ and $30(50) + 30(20)$ are equivalent. We say that $30(50 + 20)$ is in **factored form** and $30(50) + 30(20)$ is in **expanded form**.

1. Use the drawings below to answer parts a–d.

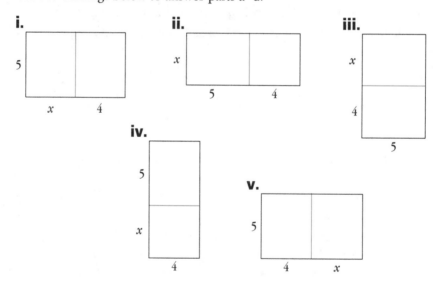

i. 5, x, 4
ii. x, 5, 4
iii. x, 4, 5
iv. 5, x, 4
v. 5, 4, x

   a. Which of the rectangles have an area of $5(4 + x)$?

   b. Write an expression in expanded form that is equivalent to $5(4 + x)$. Explain how you know that your expression is equivalent to $5(4 + x)$.

   c. Which of the rectangles have an area of $5x + 4x$?

   d. Write an expression in factored form that is equivalent to $5x + 4x$. Explain how you know that your expression is equivalent to $5x + 4x$.

2. a. Draw a diagram that uses areas of rectangles to illustrate that $5x + 10$ and $5(x + 2)$ are equivalent.

  b. Use tables or graphs to show that $5x + 10$ and $5(x + 2)$ are equivalent.

3. Write an expression in expanded form that is equivalent to the given expression. Draw a diagram to illustrate the equivalence.

  a. $1.5(4 + x)$

  b. $x(3 + 5)$

4. Write an expression in factored form that is equivalent to the given expression. Draw a diagram to illustrate the equivalence.

  a. $27 + 36x$

  b. $2x + 7x$

5. Express the area of the purple rectangle in both factored form and expanded form.

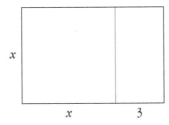

6. a. Draw a rectangle whose area can be represented by the expression $x(5 + x)$.

  b. Write an expression in expanded form that is equivalent to $x(5 + x)$.

7. As you worked on the border-tile and pool-area problems in this investigation, you found equivalent ways to express a quantity.

  a. Use what you have learned to write some expressions that are equivalent to $4x + 6$.

  b. Use what you have learned to write some expressions that are equivalent to $x^2 + 4x$.

  c. What general rules have you discovered that can help you write equivalent expressions?

As you work on these ACE questions, use your calculator whenever you need it.

Applications

1. a. How many 1-foot-square tiles are needed to form a border for a pool that is 10 feet long and 5 feet wide?

b. Write an expression for the number of border tiles needed for a pool that is *L* feet long and *W* feet wide.

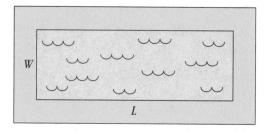

c. Write a different expression for the number of tiles needed. Explain why your expressions are equivalent.

2. A square hot tub has sides of length *s* feet. A border is created by placing square tiles measuring 1 foot on each side along the edges of the tub and triangular tiles in the corners. The triangular tiles were made by cutting square tiles in half.

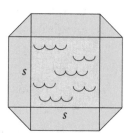

a. If the hot tub has sides of length 7 feet, how many square tiles are needed to make the border?

b. Write two equations for the number of square tiles, *N*, needed to build this type of border for a square tub with sides of length *s* feet.

3. A rectangular pool is *L* feet long and *W* feet wide. A border is created by placing square tiles measuring 1 foot on each side along the edges of the pool and triangular tiles in the corners. The triangular tiles were made by cutting square tiles in half.

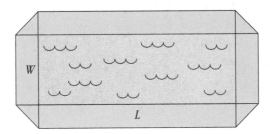

    a. If the pool is 30 feet long and 20 feet wide, how many square tiles are needed to make the border?

    b. Write two equations for the number of square tiles, *N*, needed to make this type of border for a pool *L* feet long and *W* feet wide.

In 4 and 5, write two expressions, one in factored form and one in expanded form, for the area of the purple rectangle.

4.

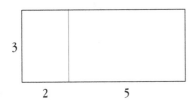

5.

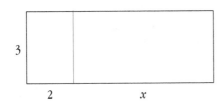

6. **a.** Which rectangles below have an area of $6(x + 1)$?

b. Write an expression in expanded form that is equivalent to $6(x + 1)$.

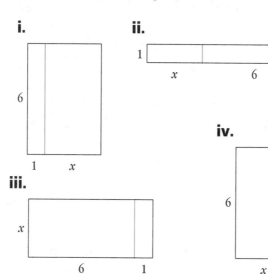

i.

ii.

iii.

iv.

7. **a.** Which rectangles below have an area of $5(2x)$? Explain your answer.

b. Write an expression that is equivalent to $5(2x)$.

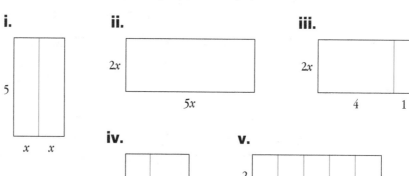

i.

ii.

iii.

iv.

v.

8. a. Is $3x + 8$ equivalent to $3(x + 8)$? Explain.

   b. Is $3(x + 8)$ equivalent to $3(8 + x)$? Explain.

   c. Is $3x + 8$ equivalent to $8 + 3x$? Explain.

In 9–12, write an expression that is equivalent to the given expression. If the given expression is in factored form, write an expression in expanded form. If the given expression is in expanded form, write an expression in factored form. Draw a diagram to illustrate the equivalence.

9. $4(x + 1)$ **10.** $16x + 8$

11. $3(2x + 5)$ **12.** $x^2 + 3x$

In 13–18, tell whether the expressions are equivalent, and explain how you know.

13. $2x + 11x$ and $13x$ **14.** $x + 3.5x$ and $3.5x$

15. $5(x + 12)$ and $5x + 12$ **16.** $7x$ and $6x + x$

17. $2L + 12$ and $2(1 + L + 5)$ **18.** $3R + 7 + 5R$ and $8R + 7$

19. Franklin's younger sister Taj and her friend Meredith are selling cookies for their girls' club. The cookies sell for $2.50 a box. For each case below, show two methods for calculating the girls' combined income.

   a. Taj sells 76 boxes and Meredith sells 49 boxes.

   b. Taj sells 43 boxes and Meredith sells 57 boxes.

   c. Taj sells x boxes and Meredith sells y boxes.

20. Sanjay did the following calculation to compute the surface area of the water in his swimming pool:

$$\text{surface area} = 20(30 + 15) = 20(45) = 900 \text{ m}^2$$

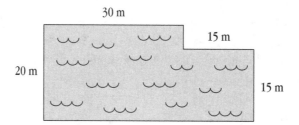

Is Sanjay's calculation correct? If so, explain his reasoning. If not, explain the mistake in his thinking.

Connections

21. A square has sides of length x centimeters. A new rectangle is created by increasing one dimension of the square by 2 centimeters and increasing the other dimension by 3 centimeters. Write two equivalent expressions, one in factored form and one in expanded form, for the area of the new rectangle. Draw a picture to illustrate the equivalence.

22. Write two expressions, one in factored form and one in expanded form, for the area of the purple rectangle below.

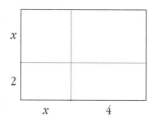

23. A circular hot tub with a radius of 4 feet is surrounded by a border 1 foot wide.

    a. What is the surface area of the water?

    b. What is the area of the border?

    c. Write an expression for the surface area of the water in a circular pool with a radius of r feet.

    d. Write an expression for the area of a 1-foot border around a circular pool with a radius of r feet.

24. The dimensions of the pool below are in feet.

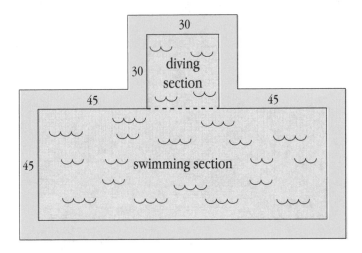

    a. How many square tiles measuring 1 foot on a side are needed to create a border for the pool?

    b. What is the surface area of the water?

    c. The swimming section is 4 feet deep and the diving section is 10 feet deep. What is the volume of the pool?

    d. The pool is filled at the rate of 600 cubic feet per hour. How long does it take to fill the pool?

Extensions

25. Susan wanted to write an expression for the number of tiles needed to make a border for a square pool with sides of length s feet. She made a table for pools with sides of length 1, 2, 3, 4, and 5 feet and used a pattern in her table to write the expression $8 + 4(s - 1)$.

Side length	1	2	3	4	5
Tiles needed	8	12	16	20	24

a. What pattern did Susan see in her table?

b. Is Susan's expression for the number of tiles equivalent to Takashi's expression in Problem 2.2? Explain why or why not.

Mathematical Reflections

In this investigation, you looked at situations that could be described by different, but equivalent, expressions. These questions will help you summarize what you have learned:

1 What do we mean when we say that the expressions $4n + 4$ and $4(n + 1)$ are *equivalent*? Make a diagram, a table, and a graph to illustrate that the expressions are equivalent.

2 **a.** Write $5x + 8x$ in factored form.

   b. Write $5(x + 7)$ in expanded form.

   c. How can you tell whether an expression is in expanded form or factored form?

3 **a.** Use drawings, graphs, tables, or some other method to show that $5(2x)$ is equivalent to $2x(5)$.

   b. Use drawings, graphs, tables, or some other method to show that $5 + 2x$ is equivalent to $2x + 5$.

   c. Make a drawing to show why $5(10) + 2$ is equivalent to $50 + 2$ but not equivalent to $5(10 + 2)$.

4 As you worked with equivalent expressions in this investigation, what patterns did you observe that you could use to show that other expressions are equivalent?

Think about your answers to these questions, discuss your ideas with other students and your teacher, and then write a summary of your findings in your journal.

Some Important Properties

In the last investigation, you used areas of rectangles to help you find equivalent expressions. The rectangle below, for example, illustrates that $4(5 + x) = 20 + 4x$.

This example illustrates an important property of the real number system called the **distributive property**. You can use the distributive property in two ways:

1. If an expression is written as a factor multiplied by a sum, you can use the distributive property to *multiply* the factor by each term in the sum.

$$4(5 + x) = 4(5) + 4x = 20 + 4x$$

2. If an expression is written as a sum of terms and the terms have a common factor, you can use the distributive property to rewrite the expression as the common factor multiplied by a sum. This process is called *factoring*.

$$20 + 4x = 4(5) + 4x = 4(5 + x)$$

The diagram below illustrates the two ways of applying the distributive property.

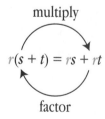

multiply

$$r(s + t) = rs + rt$$

factor

Brenda says that because subtracting a number is the same as adding its opposite, you can use the distributive property to rewrite expressions involving differences. She gave this example:

$$5(x - 2) = 5(x + {}^-2)$$
$$= 5(x) + 5({}^-2)$$
$$= 5x + {}^-10$$
$$= 5x - 10$$

Can you explain each step in Brenda's example?

The equations $2x + 10 = 10 + 2x$ and $2(x + 5) = (x + 5)2$ illustrate two other important properties. The **commutative property of addition** says that the order in which two quantities are added does not matter. The **commutative property of multiplication** says that the order in which two quantities are multiplied does not matter. These properties can be written using symbols as

$$a + b = b + a \quad \text{and} \quad ab = ba.$$

These properties are sometimes called the **rearrangement property of addition** and the **rearrangement property of multiplication**.

The distributive and commutative properties are useful for writing equivalent expressions. The distributive property allows you to rewrite expressions that involve combinations of multiplication and addition or subtraction. The commutative properties allow you to reorder the terms in an expression so you can group like terms. In this investigation, you will use these properties to solve some interesting problems.

Walking Together

Leanne, Gilberto, and Alana are participating in a walkathon to raise money for a local hospital. Each participant must find sponsors to pledge a certain amount of money per mile walked.

- Leanne asks her sponsors to pledge $1 for each mile she walks.
- Gilberto asks his sponsors to pledge $2 for each mile he walks.
- Alana asks her sponsors to pledge $5 plus $0.50 for each mile she walks.

The amount raised by each student will depend on the number of sponsors the student has and the number of miles the student walks.

Problem 3.1

The walkathon organizers have offered a prize to the three-person team that raises the most money. Leanne, Gilberto, and Alana will walk together and combine their earnings to compete for the prize. On the day of the walkathon, Leanne has pledges from 16 sponsors, Gilberto has pledges from 7 sponsors, and Alana has pledges from 11 sponsors.

A. For each student, write an equation for the amount of money the student will raise if he or she walks x miles. Then write an equation for the total amount the three-person team will raise if they walk x miles.

A_{Leanne} = _____

$A_{Gilberto}$ = _____

A_{Alana} = _____

A_{total} = _____

B. Alana asked each of her 11 sponsors to pledge $5 in addition to an amount per mile, so the team will raise $55 regardless of how far they walk.

  1. Excluding the $55, how much will the team raise per mile?

  2. Use your answer from part 1 to help you write a different equation for the total amount the team will raise if they walk x miles.

C. 1. Use the distributive and commutative properties to show that the two expressions you wrote for the total amount the team will raise are equivalent.

  2. Verify that the expressions are equivalent by making and comparing tables or graphs.

■ Problem 3.1 Follow-Up

In Problem 3.1, you used the distributive and commutative properties to write equivalent expressions for the amount of money the team will raise. The context of the problem may have helped you understand why these properties make sense. Now you will practice applying the properties to algebraic expressions that are not in context.

In 1–12, tell whether the expressions are equivalent, and explain your reasoning.

1. $3x + 5x$ and $8x$

2. $3x + 5$ and $8x$

3. $4(x + 7)$ and $4x + 7$

4. $5(x + 2)$ and $5x + 10$

5. $12 + 8x$ and $4(3 + 2x)$

6. $4x + x + 2x$ and $8x$

7. $7 + 5x$ and $5x + 7$

8. $3x + 8$ and $8x + 3$

9. $5x + 3x + 4x$ and $4x + 5x + 3x$

10. $6 + 2t$ and $2(t + 3)$

11. $2(L + 2) + 2W$ and $2L + 2W + 4$

12. $2L + 2W + 4$ and $2(L + W + 2)$

3.2 Estimating Profit

At their planning meeting, the organizers of the hospital walkathon discussed expenses and income. They made the following estimates:

- Expense for posters and newspaper, radio, and TV ads: $500
- Expense for souvenir T-shirts for participants: $6 per child, $8.50 per adult
- Income from business sponsors whose logos will appear on T-shirts and signs: $1000
- Expense for paramedics and an ambulance in case of emergency: $250
- Income from registration fees: $5 per child, $15 per adult

Notice that some of the expenses are fixed, while others depend on the number of adults and children who participate. The difference between the total income and the total expenses is the profit. The organizers will donate any profit from the event to the hospital.

A. Estimate the total income, the total expenses, and the total profit if 40 children and 30 adults participate in the walkathon.

B. Write two equivalent expressions for the total income in terms of the number of adults, *a*, and the number of children, *c*, who participate.

C. Write two equivalent expressions for the total expenses in terms of the number of adults, *a*, and the number of children, *c*, who participate.

D. Use parentheses and your results from parts B and C to write an expression showing the profit as total income minus total expenses. That is, express the profit as (expression for income) − (expression for expenses).

E. Write an expression for profit that is equivalent to your expression from part D but that is as short as possible. Use the distributive and commutative properties to show that the two profit expressions are equivalent.

F. Evaluate your profit expressions from parts D and E for $a = 100$ and $c = 75$. Can you conclude from your results that the expressions are equivalent? Explain.

G. Compare the profit expressions you wrote in parts D and E. What are the advantages and disadvantages of writing the profit expression in a shorter form?

Problem 3.2 Follow-Up

In Problem 3.2, you might have written this expression for profit:

$$(1000 + 5c + 15a) - (500 + 6c + 8.50a + 250)$$

The first pair of parentheses in this expression can be deleted, but to remove the second pair, you must *distribute* the minus sign to each term within the parentheses.

$$(1000 + 5c + 15a) - (500 + 6c + 8.50a + 250) = 1000 + 5c + 15a - 500 - 6c - 8.50a - 250$$

Distributing the minus sign to each term is a special case of the distributive property.

$$^-(s + t) = {}^-1(s + t) = {}^-1(s) + {}^-1(t) = {}^-s + {}^-t = {}^-s - t$$

1. Benjamin's math test consisted of 10 questions, each worth 5 points. Benjamin answered two questions incorrectly. Show at least two ways to calculate his score.

2. **a.** Describe a situation that can be represented by the expression $100 - (x + y)$. Explain what x and y represent in your situation.

   b. Use the distributive property to help you write an expression that is equivalent to $100 - (x + y)$.

3. **a.** Describe a situation that can be represented by the expression $50 - 2x - 2y$. Explain what x and y represent in your situation.

   b. Use the distributive property to help you write an expression that is equivalent to $50 - 2x - 2y$.

4. The expression $3 + 2x$ is equivalent to $2x + 3$. Is $3 - 2x$ equivalent to $2x - 3$? Explain why or why not.

5. Apply the properties you have learned in this investigation to simplify each expression.
   a. $(9x + 15) - (8 + 2x)$
   b. $(7x - 12) - (9x + 15)$
   c. $(14r + 9t + 15) + (23 - 9r + 3t)$
   d. $19 - 12x + 20 + 9x$

3.3 Finding the Area of a Trapezoid

The figure below is a trapezoid. A *trapezoid* is a quadrilateral with one pair of parallel sides. The parallel sides, labeled *a* and *b*, are called the *bases* of the trapezoid. The distance from side *a* to side *b*, labeled *h*, is the *height*.

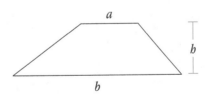

Ms. Ochoa's students have learned how to find areas of triangles, rectangles, and parallelograms. Now, Ms. Ochoa has challenged her students to find a method for calculating the area of a trapezoid.

Tua, Sam, and Carlos have found three methods for calculating the area. Each method involves dividing and rearranging the trapezoid into other shapes.

Problem 3.3

The students made drawings to illustrate their methods for calculating the area of a trapezoid. Try to figure out how each student thought about the problem.

Tua's method

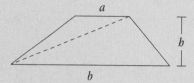

Sam's method

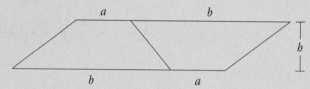

Carlos's method

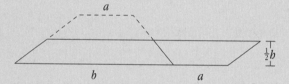

A. Explain each student's method for finding the area.

B. Write an algebraic expression to describe each method.

C. Show that the expressions you wrote in part B are equivalent.

■ Problem 3.3 Follow-Up

1. a. Natasha lost her drawing, but she had written this expression for finding the area of a trapezoid:

$$\tfrac{1}{2}h(b - a) + ha$$

Use this expression to decide what Natasha's drawing might have looked like. Make a drawing, and use it to help explain Natasha's method for finding the area.

b. Is Natasha's expression equivalent to the three expressions in part B? Explain.

2. A trapezoid has a height of 10 centimeters and bases of 9 centimeters and 15 centimeters. Find the area of the trapezoid using each of the four expressions.

3.4 Writing Quadratic Expressions

In your work in this unit, you have discovered that a situation can often be represented by different, but equivalent, algebraic expressions. Most of the expressions you have worked with have been linear expressions. In this problem, you will practice finding equivalent *quadratic* expressions.

The table below shows the results of the games played by a five-team soccer league. Each team played each of the other teams twice—once at home and once away. A *W* means the home team won the game; an *L* means the home team lost. For example, the Alligators won their home game against the Cats, but they lost when they played on the Cats' home field. What do the "—" symbols mean? How many games were played in all?

		Visiting Team				
		Alligators	Buzzards	Cats	Ducks	Elks
Home Team	Alligators	—	W	W	L	W
	Buzzards	L	—	L	L	W
	Cats	W	W	—	L	L
	Ducks	W	W	W	—	W
	Elks	L	W	W	W	—

Problem 3.4

In parts A–C, you will explore three ways of thinking about this question: If a league has n teams and each team plays each of the other teams twice, how many games are played in all?

A. Figure out how many games would be played for leagues with 2, 3, 4, 5, and 6 teams. Record your results in a table similar to the one below.

Number of teams	2	3	4	5	6
Number of games					

Look for a pattern in your table. Use the pattern to write an expression for the number of games played by a league with n teams.

B. Suppose a sports reporter wants to attend exactly one game in the schedule of an n-team league.

  1. How many choices does the reporter have for the home team for the game she attends?

  2. Once she has chosen a home team, how many choices does she have for the visiting team?

  3. Use your answers from parts 1 and 2 to write an expression for the total number of games the reporter can choose from.

C. Suppose you made a table similar to the one on page 41 to record wins and losses for an n-team league.

  1. How many cells would your table have?

  2. How many cells in the table would not be used for W or L entries?

  3. Use your answers from parts 1 and 2 to write an expression for the total number of games played.

D. In parts A–C, you wrote expressions for the number of games played by an n-team league. Show that these expressions are equivalent.

■ Problem 3.4 Follow-Up

Many quadratic expressions can be written in both factored form and expanded form. The area of the purple rectangle below can be written as $x^2 + 3x$ or as $x(x + 3)$.

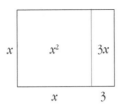

You can use the distributive property to show the equivalence of the factored and expanded forms of a quadratic expression. For example, you can change $x^2 + 3x$ to $x(x + 3)$ by factoring an x from each term. You can change $x(x + 3)$ to $x^2 + 3x$ by multiplying each term by x.

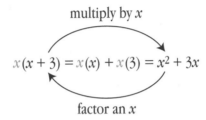

multiply by x

$$x(x + 3) = x(x) + x(3) = x^2 + 3x$$

factor an x

You can apply the distributive property to more complex factored expressions. This example shows how you can change the factored expression $(x + 2)(x + 3)$ to expanded form by applying the distributive property several times.

$$
\begin{aligned}
(x + 2)(x + 3) &= (x + 2)x + (x + 2)3 && \text{Multiply } (x + 2) \text{ by each term of } x + 3. \\
&= x^2 + 2x + (x + 2)3 && \text{Multiply } x \text{ by each term of } x + 2. \\
&= x^2 + 2x + 3x + 6 && \text{Multiply } 3 \text{ by each term of } x + 2. \\
&= x^2 + 5x + 6 && \text{Combine like terms.}
\end{aligned}
$$

Writing an expanded quadratic expression in factored form often poses more difficult challenges. You will learn more about factoring quadratic expressions in future math classes.

In 1–6, use the distributive property to find an expression that is equivalent to the given expression. Check each answer by using your calculator to compare tables and graphs.

1. $x(^-4x + 3)$ **2.** $(4x + 3)(x + 7)$ **3.** $(x - 4.5)(x + 6.5)$

4. $(2x - 5)(5x - 2)$ **5.** $x^2 - 6x$ **6.** $12x - 3x^2$

7. Look at your reasoning and your results from questions 1–6.
  a. Describe any general rules you discover for multiplying two linear factors.
  b. Describe any general rules you discover for factoring a quadratic expression.

As you work on these ACE questions, use your calculator whenever you need it.

Applications

1. **a.** Write an expression that is equivalent to $3x - (4 + 2x)$.

    b. Evaluate $3x - (4 + 2x)$ and the expression you wrote for $x = 5$ and $x = {}^-1$.

2. **a.** Write an expression that is equivalent to $3(x + 2) + 2(x + 2)$.

    b. Evaluate $3(x + 2) + 2(x + 2)$ and the expression you wrote for $x = 5$ and $x = {}^-1$.

3. **a.** Write an expression that is equivalent to $3(x + 2) - 2(x + 2)$.

    b. Evaluate $3(x + 2) - 2(x + 2)$ and the expression you wrote for $x = 5$ and $x = {}^-1$.

In 4–9, use the distributive and commutative properties to write two expressions that are equivalent to the given expression. Then tell which of the three expressions is easiest to evaluate for a given x value.

4. $3x + 2 + 5x$

5. $12 - 8x + 15 + 10x$

6. $(3x^2 + 5x + 8) + (9x^2 + 2x - 7)$

7. $(5 - 7x) - 2(5x + 12)$

8. $7(4x - 2) + 3(5 + 2x)$

9. $(3x^2 + 5x + 8) - (9x^2 + 2x - 7)$

10. **a.** Evaluate the expression $5000 - 50(75 - T)$ for $T = 25$. Describe the order in which you performed the operations.

    b. Write an expression that is equivalent to $5000 - 50(75 - T)$, and evaluate your expression for $T = 25$. Did the order in which you performed the operations change? Explain.

    c. Which expression is easier to evaluate?

11. Describe a real-life situation you could use to convince someone that $2x + 5x$ and $7x$ are different ways of expressing the same information.

12. Describe a real-life situation you could use to convince someone that $3x + 5 + 4x$ and $7x + 5$ are different ways of expressing the same information.

In 13–18, copy the statement and insert parentheses, if needed, to make the statement true. For example, to make $3x + 1 - 2x = x + 3$ a true statement, you could write $3(x + 1) - 2x = x + 3$.

13. $6x - 4x - 3x = 5x$

14. $6x - 4x - 3x = {}^-x$

15. $7 + 5p - p = 11p$

16. $7 + 5p - p = 7$

17. $7 + 5p - p = 7 + 4p$

18. $7 + 5p - p = 0$

In 19 and 20, copy the statement, replacing the question mark with a number or an expression that makes the statement true.

19. $2(4 + ?) = 18$

20. $2(4 + ?) = 8 + 6x$

21. **a.** Write 12 as a product of two factors and as a product of three factors.

    b. Write 12 as a sum of two terms and as a sum of three terms.

    c. Write 12 as a product of two factors in which one of the factors is the sum of two terms.

Connections

In 22–24, write two expressions, one in factored form and one in expanded form, for the area of the purple rectangle. Show how the equivalence of the two expressions illustrates the distributive property.

22.

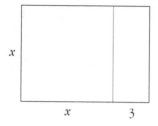

23.

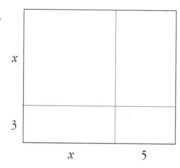

24.

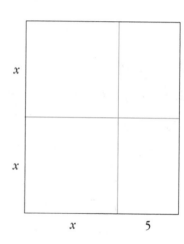

In 25–29, do parts a–c.

25. $^{-}3x + 6 + 5x$ and $6 + 2x$

26. $10 - 5x$ and $5x - 10$

27. $(3x + 4) + (2x - 3)$ and $5x + 1$

28. $9x - 5(x - 3) - 20$ and $5 - 4x$

29. $(10x - 5) - (4x + 2)$ and $10x - 5 - 4x + 2$

    a. Make a table and a graph for the two expressions. Show x values from $^{-}5$ to 5 on the graph.

    b. Based on your table and graph, tell whether you think the expressions are equivalent.

c. If you think the expressions are equivalent, use the commutative and distributive properties to verify their equivalence. If you think they are not equivalent, use the properties to show why.

In 30–32, use the distributive property to show that the expressions are equivalent. Draw a rectangle to illustrate their equivalence.

30. $x(x + 5)$ and $x^2 + 5x$

31. $(2 + x)(2 + 3x)$ and $4 + 8x + 3x^2$

32. $(x + 2)(2x + 3)$ and $2x^2 + 7x + 6$

33. You have seen that many quadratic expressions can be written in factored form and in expanded form.

   a. Which form would you use to determine whether a quadratic relationship has a maximum point or a minimum point? Why?

   b. Which form would you use to find the x- and y-intercepts of a quadratic relationship? Why?

   c. Which form would you use to find the line of symmetry for a quadratic relationship? Why?

   d. Which form would you use to find the coordinates of the maximum or minimum point for a quadratic relationship? Why?

34. For each pair of expressions in questions 30–32, there is an associated quadratic relationship. For example, the expressions in question 30 are associated with the relationship $y = x(x + 5)$, or $y = x^2 + 5x$. Do parts a–c for each pair of expressions in questions 30–32.

   a. Find the x- and y-intercepts of the associated quadratic relationship.

   b. Find the line of symmetry.

   c. Find the coordinates of the maximum or minimum point.

   d. Sketch the graph and indicate the information from parts a–c.

In 35–37, tell whether the expressions are equivalent. If they are, use the distributive and commutative properties to illustrate their equivalence. If they are not equivalent, explain why not.

35. $5x^2 + x$ and $x(5x + 1)$

36. $3x^2 + 15$ and $3x(x + 15)$

37. $^-4x + 12x^2$ and $^-4x(1 - 3x)$

38. Data from past seasons show that the number of people who visit Water Works park on a given day depends on the day's high temperature. The manager wrote the equation $V = 200 + 50(T - 70)$ to estimate the number of visitors based on the day's predicted high temperature, T, in degrees Fahrenheit.

a. What sequence of operations do you need to perform to find the expected number of visitors for a given temperature?

b. Use the commutative and distributive properties to find a different equation for the number of visitors as a function of the temperature.

c. Describe how the expected number of visitors changes as the temperature increases.

d. Without using the table feature of your calculator, estimate the number of visitors on a day when the predicted high temperature is 83°F.

e. Estimate the number of visitors on a day when the predicted high temperature is 68°F and on a day when the predicted high temperature is 65°F. What do your answers indicate about the limitations of this equation model?

f. In parts c–e, which equation did you use to calculate your answers? Explain why you chose this equation.

39. Suppose D dollars are invested in a money-market account that earns 10% interest per year. If no money is withdrawn, the amount of money in the account at the end of one year is $D + 0.10D$.

    a. Write an equivalent expression in factored form.

    b. If $1500 is invested, how much money will be in the account at the end of the first year?

40. **a.** Write an expression for the total price of an item that costs P dollars plus 6% sales tax.

    b. What is the total price of a jacket that costs $47 plus 6% sales tax?

41. **a.** A store is offering a 30% discount on all purchases. Write an expression for the discounted price of an item that normally sells for P dollars.

    b. What is the discounted price of a pair of hiking boots that normally sells for $68.50?

42. A tour operator's total expense for a bus tour with N people is $200 + 10N$. The tour operator charges each person $30.

    a. Write two equivalent expressions for the profit the tour operator will earn if N people go on the tour.

    b. What will the profit be if 10 people go on the tour? If 75 people go?

    c. How many people must go on the tour for the tour operator to break even? Explain.

    d. Write an expression for the average per-person profit the operator will earn.

Extensions

In 43–45, tell whether the expressions are equivalent. If they are, use the distributive and commutative properties to illustrate their equivalence.

43. $x^2 + 5x + 4$ and $(x + 1)(x + 4)$

44. $3x^2 + 15x$ and $3x(x + 15)$

45. $(x - 5)(x + 2)$ and $x^2 - 3x - 10$

In 46 and 47, use this information: In Problem 3.2, you may have written the following expression for the estimated profit from the walkathon:

$$(1000 + 5c + 15a) - (500 + 6c + 8.50a + 250)$$

An equivalent expression in simplified form is this:

$$250 - c + 6.50a$$

46. When Marcel simplified the profit expression, he found a different result. Study the steps in his reasoning, and find his mistake.

$$
\begin{aligned}
(1000 + 5c + 15a) &- (500 + 6c + 8.50a + 250) \\
&= 1000 + 5c + 15a - 500 + 6c + 8.50a + 250 \\
&= 1000 - 500 + 250 + 5c + 6c + 15a + 8.50a \\
&= 750 + 11c + 23.50a
\end{aligned}
$$

47. Kirtee found a different simplified expression. Study the steps in her reasoning, and find her mistake.

$$
\begin{aligned}
(1000 + 5c + 15a) &- (500 + 6c + 8.50a + 250) \\
&= 1000 + 5c + 15a - 500 - 6c - 8.50a - 250 \\
&= 1000 - 500 - 250 + 5c - 6c + 15a - 8.50a \\
&= 250 + c + 6.50a
\end{aligned}
$$

In 48–51, rewrite the expression so that the calculation is easy to do in your head. Then perform the calculation mentally, and check the result with your calculator.

48. $7(25) + 7(75)$ **49.** $9(4) + 11(4)$

50. $3(99) + 3(101)$ **51.** $5(106)$

In 52–57, use the distributive and commutative properties to simplify each expression as much as possible. Check that the original expression and your simplified expression are equivalent by testing several x values in both expressions.

52. $2(9x + 15) - (8 + 2x)$

53. $(7x - 12) - 2(3x + 10)$

54. $(19 - 12x) - (^-9x - 20)$

55. $2[3x + 5(x + 1)] - (10x + 2)$

56. $4 - 2(3x + 5) - (^-10 - 6x) - 4$

57. $(3x + 1)(2x - 3) - (1 - x)(1 - 6x)$

Mathematical Reflections

In this investigation, you used the distributive and commutative properties to write equivalent expressions. These questions will help you summarize what you have learned:

1 Explain how the distributive and commutative properties can be used to write equivalent expressions. Use examples to illustrate your explanations.

2 a. Give an example of a real-life situation that can be represented by at least two equivalent expressions. Explain how each expression represents the situation.

b. Use the distributive and commutative properties to show that the expressions are equivalent.

Think about your answers to these questions, discuss your ideas with other students and your teacher, and then write a summary of your findings in your journal.

INVESTIGATION 4

Solving Equations

Solving mathematical problems often requires finding solutions to equations or inequalities. In this investigation, you will learn algebraic methods for solving linear and quadratic equations.

4.1 Comparing Costs

Imagine that you are a member of a creative-writing club. The club wants to publish a book of students' short stories, poems, and essays. You contact two local printers to obtain bids on the cost of printing the books.

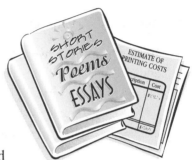

bid 1: cost = $100 + $4 × the number of books printed
bid 2: cost = $25 + $7 × the number of books printed

In earlier units, you learned strategies for comparing the two bids. If you let x represent the number of books printed and y represent the cost in dollars, the equations become $y = 100 + 4x$ and $y = 25 + 7x$. You can use your graphing calculator to make and compare tables and graphs of these equations.

> ### Problem 4.1
>
> Use your graphing calculator to help answer parts A–C.
>
> **A.** Make a table of x and y values for each bid. Use your table to find the number of books for which the two bids are equal. Explain your work.
>
> **B.** Make a graph of the two equations. Use your graph to find the number of books for which the two bids are equal. Copy the graph onto your paper, and use it to help explain how you found your answer.
>
> **C.** For what numbers of books is bid 1 less than bid 2? Explain how you found your answer.

1. For each bid, find the cost of printing 75 books. Explain how you found your answers.

2. For each bid, find the greatest number of books that can be printed if the cost is not to exceed $300. Explain your answers.

3. The club decides to request bids from two more printers.

bid 3: cost = $8 × the number of books printed
bid 4: cost = $30 + $6 × the number of books printed

For what number of books are these two bids equal? Explain how you found your answer.

4.2 Solving Linear Equations

You know how to solve equations by using your calculator to make and compare graphs and tables. However, you can solve many equations without using a calculator by operating on the symbols. In Problem 4.1, the equation for bid 1 is $y = 100 + 4x$, where y is the cost and x is the number of books printed. To find out how many books can be printed for $300, you can solve the equation $300 = 100 + 4x$ for the variable x.

In your earlier mathematics work, you learned that to solve linear equations such as $300 = 100 + 4x$, you need to *undo* the mathematical operations until x is alone on one side of the equation. To make sure the sides of the equation remain equal, you must apply any mathematical operation to *both* sides. This *symbolic method* of solution is illustrated in the example below.

$$300 = 100 + 4x$$
$$300 - 100 = 100 - 100 + 4x \quad \text{Since 100 is added to } 4x, \text{ subtract 100 from}$$
$$200 = 4x \qquad\qquad\quad \textit{both sides} \text{ of the equation.}$$

$$\frac{200}{4} = \frac{4x}{4} \qquad\qquad \text{Since } x \text{ is multiplied by 4, divide } \textit{both sides} \text{ by 4.}$$

$$50 = x \qquad\qquad\quad \text{Now } x \text{ is alone on one side of the equation. It is}$$
easy to see that the solution is 50. This means that 50 books can be printed for $300.

In Problem 4.1, you found the number of books for which the two bids are equal. This is the same as solving the equation $100 + 4x = 25 + 7x$ for the variable x. Unlike the previous example, this equation has an x on both sides. However, the method for solving the equation is the same: *undo* the mathematical operations until the variable is alone on one side of the equation, making sure to apply all mathematical operations to *both sides* of the equation.

The example below shows one way to solve the equation $100 + 4x = 25 + 7x$.

$$100 + 4x = 25 + 7x$$
$$100 + 4x - 4x = 25 + 7x - 4x \qquad \text{1.}$$
$$100 = 25 + 3x$$
$$100 - 25 = 25 + 3x - 25 \qquad \text{2.}$$
$$75 = 3x$$
$$\frac{75}{3} = \frac{3x}{3} \qquad \text{3.}$$
$$25 = x$$

A. Supply an explanation for each numbered step in the above solution to $100 + 4x = 25 + 7x$.

B. The solution above begins by subtracting $4x$ from both sides of the equation. Show a solution that begins with a different step.

C. How can you check that $x = 25$ is the correct solution? Show that your method works.

■ Problem 4.2 Follow-Up

Solutions to linear equations are often given in fewer steps, with some of the details omitted. It is assumed that the reader can fill in the gaps. In this solution to $11x - 12 = 30 + 5x$, some of the details have been omitted.

$$11x - 12 = 30 + 5x$$
$$11x = 42 + 5x$$
$$6x = 42$$
$$x = 7$$

1. Copy the solution above, filling in the details that were omitted.

2. How can you check that $x = 7$ is the correct solution? Demonstrate your method.

3. Explain how you could use a graph and a table to solve the equation $11x - 12 = 30 + 5x$.

Reasoning with Symbols

Although you can solve equations by making tables or graphs, it is often more efficient to use the symbolic method described in Problem 4.2.

Problem 4.3

In A–D, use the symbolic method to solve the equation.

A. $7x + 15 = 12x + 5$ **B.** $14 - 3x = 1.5x + 5$

C. $^-3x + 5 = 2x - 10$ **D.** $3 + 5(x + 2) = 7x - 1$

E. Check your solutions to the equations in A–D.

F. Look over your work for A–D. Record any general strategies that seem to work well in solving linear equations.

■ Problem 4.3 Follow-Up

1. In a–c, the given equation is related to the equation $y = 7.5x - 23.5$. Explain what question the solution to the given equation answers. For example, the solution to $7.5x - 23.5 = 10$ answers the question "What is the value of x in the equation $y = 7.5x - 23.5$ when $y = 10$?" Then use a table or a graph to solve the equation, and explain how you found your solution.

     a. $7.5x - 23.5 = 51.5$ **b.** $7.5x - 23.5 = 0$ **c.** $7.5x - 23.5 = ^-30$

2. Write a linear equation with a solution of $x = 2$. Do you think everyone in your class wrote the same equation? Explain.

3. The school choir is selling boxes of greeting cards to raise money for a trip. The equation for the profit in dollars, P, in terms of the number of boxes sold, x, is

$$P = 3x - (100 + 2x).$$

     a. How many boxes must the choir sell to make a $200 profit? Explain how you found your answer.

     b. How many boxes must the choir sell to break even? Explain how you found your answer.

4.4 Solving Quadratic Equations

Different ways of thinking about a problem can lead to different methods for solving it. For example, finding the x-intercepts of the graph of $y = x^2 + 5x$ is the same as solving the equation $x^2 + 5x = 0$.

In earlier units, you solved quadratic equations by using tables and graphs. For example, to solve $x^2 + 5x = 0$, you can trace a graph of $y = x^2 + 5x$ to find x values for which $y = 0$. Or you can make a table of values and look for the x values that correspond to a y value of 0.

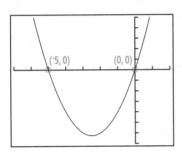

x	y
$^-7$	14
$^-6$	6
$^-5$	0
$^-4$	$^-4$
$^-3$	$^-6$
$^-2$	$^-6$
$^-1$	$^-4$
0	0
1	6
2	14
3	24

The solutions to $x^2 + 5x = 0$ are called the **roots** of the equation $y = x^2 + 5x$. A quadratic equation may have zero, one, or two roots. If r is a root of an equation, then the point $(r, 0)$ is an x-intercept of the graph.

Algebra provides important tools that can help you solve quadratic equations such as $x^2 + 5x = 0$ without using tables or graphs. This problem illustrates a symbolic method for finding the roots of some quadratic equations.

Problem 4.4

A. The expression $x^2 + 3x$ is in expanded form. Write an equivalent expression in factored form.

B. Find all possible solutions to the equation $x^2 + 3x = 0$. Explain how you know you have found all the solutions.

C. What are the x-intercepts of $y = x^2 + 3x$? Explain how your answers to part B can help you answer this question.

D. Which form of the expression $x^2 + 3x$, the expanded form or the factored form, is more useful for finding the roots, or x-intercepts, of the equation $y = x^2 + 3x$? Explain your reasoning.

E. In 1 and 2, an equation is given for both the factored form and the expanded form of a quadratic expression. Find the roots, or x-intercepts, of the equation without making a table or a graph, and tell which form of the equation you used to find your answer.

    1. $y = 4x^2 - 8x$ or $y = 4x(x - 2)$ **2.** $y = 6x(5 - 2x)$ or $y = 30x - 12x^2$

F. In 1–3, solve the equation by first factoring the quadratic expression.

    1. $x^2 + 4.5x = 0$ **2.** $x^2 - 9x = 0$ **3.** $^-x^2 + 10x = 0$

■ Problem 4.4 Follow-Up

1. Check your answers to part F without using a table or a graph.

2. Check your answers to part F by making graphs and finding the x-intercepts.

3. **a.** For each expression below, find an equivalent expression in expanded form.
    b. Which form of the expression would you use to predict the x-intercepts of the related graph? Find the x-intercepts and explain your reasoning.
      i. $(2x + 1)(x + 5)$ **ii.** $(x + 2)(x - 2)$

4. Use the diagram below to find the linear factors of $x^2 + 8x + 12$. Use the factors to solve the equation $x^2 + 8x + 12 = 0$.

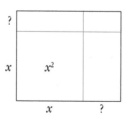

$$x^2 + 8x + 12 = (x + ?)(x + ?)$$

As you work on these ACE questions, use your calculator whenever you need it.

Applications

In 1–10, solve the equation by using the symbolic method. Check your solution by making tables or graphs with your calculator.

1. $6x + 10 = 4x + 18$

2. $3x + 47 = 7x + 7$

3. $10 - 5x = 10x + 5(x - 6)$

4. $^-13x + 36 = 20x - 30$

5. $8.3x - 10.75 = 51.5$

6. $x(x - 7) = 0$

7. $x^2 + 1.5x = 0$

8. $x^2 + 6x + 8 = 0$

9. $x^2 + 2x + 1 = 0$

10. $8x - x^2 = 0$

11. The student council is sponsoring a T-shirt sale. They plan to take orders in advance so they know how many T-shirts to have printed. They made the following estimates of expenses and income for their sale:

- Expense of $350 for advertising
- Expense of $3.25 for each T-shirt
- Income of $10 for each T-shirt
- Income of $200 from a local business in exchange for printing the business's logo on the back of the T-shirts

a. Write an equation for the profit, P, the student council will make if they sell n T-shirts.

b. How many T-shirts must the student council sell to break even? Describe at least three ways you could find the answer to this question. Use one of the ways to find the solution.

Connections

12. The equations $N = 2s + 2(s + 2)$ and $N = 4(s + 2) - 4$ represent the number of square tiles, measuring 1 foot on each side, needed to make a border for a square pool with sides of length s feet.

   a. Solve $N = 2s + 2(s + 2)$ for $N = 48$.

   b. Solve $N = 4(s + 2) - 4$ for $N = 48$.

   c. How do your answers for parts a and b compare? Why?

13. The number of visitors to a park depends on the day's high Fahrenheit temperature, T, according to the equation $V = 200 + 50(T - 70)$. If 1000 people visit the park one day, what would you predict was that day's high temperature?

14. The number of games played in a league with n teams if each team plays each of the other teams twice is $g = n^2 - n$. What are the x-intercepts of the graph of this equation? Explain what information they represent.

15. The height in feet of an arch above a point x feet from one of its bases is given by the equation $y = 0.2x(100 - x)$. What is the maximum height of the arch? Explain how you found your answer.

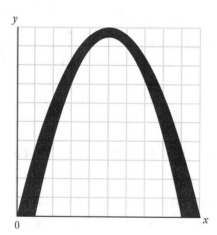

16. Below are the graphs of $y = 1.5x + 6$ and $y = {}^-2x + 15$. The scale on the x-axis is 1, and the scale on the y-axis is 3.

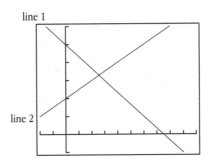

line 1

line 2

a. Match each equation, $y = 1.5x + 6$ and $y = {}^-2x + 15$, to line 1 or line 2.

b. What are the coordinates of the point of intersection of the two lines?

c. How could you find the answer to part b without using a graph or a table?

d. What values of x satisfy the inequality $1.5x + 6 < {}^-2x + 15$? How is your answer shown on the graph?

e. What values of x satisfy the inequality $1.5x + 6 > {}^-2x + 15$? How is your answer shown on the graph?

17. Below is the graph of $y = x^2 - 9x$. The scale on the x-axis is 1, and the scale on the y-axis is 2. Use the graph to answer parts a–e on the next page.

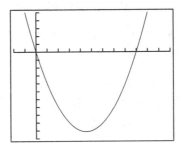

a. What are the coordinates of the x-intercepts?

b. How could you find the answer to part a without using a graph or a table?

c. What values of x satisfy the inequality $x^2 - 9x < 0$? How is your answer shown on the graph?

d. What values of x satisfy the inequality $x^2 - 9x > 0$? How is your answer shown on the graph?

e. What is the minimum y value? What x value corresponds to this minimum value?

Extensions

18. Below is the graph of $y = (x + 3)(x - 2)$. The scale on both axes is 1.

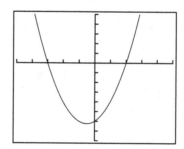

a. Solve $(x + 3)(x - 2) = 0$? How are the solutions shown on the graph?

b. What values of x satisfy the inequality $(x + 3)(x - 2) < 0$? How is your answer shown on the graph?

c. How can you find the answer to part b, without using the graph, by analyzing the inequality? (Hint: Use what you know about multiplying positive and negative numbers.)

19. Here is the graph of $y = (x + 2)(x - 1)(x - 5)$. The scale on the x-axis is 1, and the scale on the y-axis is 5.

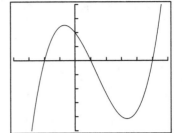

   a. Solve $(x + 2)(x - 1)(x - 5) = 0$? How are the solutions shown on the graph?

   b. What values of x satisfy the inequality $(x + 2)(x - 1)(x - 5) < 0$? How is your answer shown on the graph?

   c. How can you find the answer to part b, without using the graph, by analyzing the inequality? (Hint: Use what you know about multiplying positive and negative numbers.)

In 20 and 21, solve the equation and check your answer.

20. $5 + 8(x + 2) = 6(1 + x) - 1$

21. $2x - 3(x + 4) - 10 = 9 - 3(2 + 2x)$

22. **a.** Use an area model to find the factored form of the expression $x^2 + 7x + 12$.

   b. Use your answer to help you solve the equation $x^2 + 7x + 12 = 0$.

23. **a.** Use an area model to find the factored form of the expression $x^2 + 8x + 15$.

   b. Use your answer to help you solve the equation $x^2 + 8x + 15 = 0$.

24. **a.** Use an area model to find the factored form of the expression $x^2 - 9$.

   b. Use your answer to help you solve the equation $x^2 - 9 = 0$.

25. **a.** Use an area model to find the factored form of the expression $2x^2 + 5x + 3$.

   b. Use your answer to help you solve the equation $2x^2 + 5x + 3 = 0$.

In 26 and 27, solve the equation. Explain your reasoning.

26. $x^2 + 5x + 7 = 1$ **27.** $x^2 + 6x + 15 = 6$

Mathematical Reflections

In this investigation, you learned methods for solving linear and quadratic equations. These questions will help you summarize what you have learned:

1 Describe some general strategies for solving linear equations. Give examples that illustrate your strategies.

2 **a.** What general strategies can you use to solve quadratic equations of the form $ax^2 + bx = 0$?

b. Will the strategies you described in part a work for solving quadratic equations of the form $ax^2 + bx + c = 0$? Use an example to help explain your answer.

3 In a–c, illustrate your ideas with an example.

a. How could you solve a linear equation of the form $mx + b = 0$ by using a graph?

b. How could you solve a linear equation of the form $ax + b = cx + d$ by using a graph?

c. How could you solve a quadratic equation of the form $ax^2 + bx = 0$ by using a graph?

Think about your answers to these questions, discuss your ideas with other students and your teacher, and then write a summary of your findings in your journal.

INVESTIGATION 5

Writing Expressions for Surface Area

In this unit, you have seen that many situations can be represented by several different, but equivalent, algebraic expressions, and you have learned methods for writing equivalent expressions. You have also developed algebraic strategies for solving linear and quadratic equations. In this investigation, you will apply all the ideas you have learned.

5.1 Stacking Rods

In this problem, you will find the surface area of stacks of staggered rods.

Problem 5.1

You will need four to six rods of the same length and several unit rods. In this problem, you will find the surface area of stacks of the longer rods. The rods in each stack should be staggered by 1 unit, as shown below.

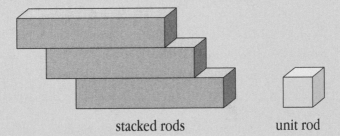

stacked rods   unit rod

A. Use the unit rods to determine the dimensions of one of the longer rods.

B. Find the surface area of a single rod, a stack of two rods, a stack of three rods, and so on.

C. Use your findings to help you write an equation for the relationship between the surface area, A, and the number of rods in the stack, N.

Problem 5.1 Follow-Up

1. Compare your expression for surface area with the expressions written by other groups who used rods of the same length.

   a. Are all the expressions equivalent? Explain why or why not by using the rules you have learned for writing equivalent expressions.

   b. Use your calculator to make a table and a graph of your equation. How could you use tables or graphs to check whether the expressions found by your group and the other groups are equivalent?

2. a. Use your equation to find the surface area of a stack of 12 rods.

   b. Use your equation to find the surface area of a stack of 20 rods.

3. Will your equation work to calculate the surface area of stacks made from rods of a different length? If not, how could you change your equation so it would work? Check your idea by looking at the equations written by groups who used rods of a different length.

4. Is the relationship between the surface area and the number of rods linear, quadratic, exponential, or none of these? Explain your answer.

As you work on these ACE questions, use your calculator whenever you need it.

Applications

1. In their work in Problem 5.1, Kwang-Hee's group used rods that are 4 units long. They wrote this equation for the surface area of a stack of N rods:

    $$A = 18 + 12(N - 1)$$

    a. Is this equation correct? Explain how you know.

    b. What is the surface area of a stack of 15 of these rods?

    c. If the surface area of a stack of these rods is 246 square units, how many rods are in the stack? Explain how you found your answer.

2. In their work in Problem 5.1, two groups in Mr. Samartino's class used rods that are 4 units long. Each group wrote an equation for the surface area of a stack of N rods.

    $$A = 18 + 12(N - 1)$$

    $$A = 4(2N + 2) + 2(2N - 1)(1)$$

    a. For each equation, describe how the group might have thought about the problem. Explain what each part of the equation represents.

    b. Show that the expressions for the surface area are equivalent.

    c. The surface area of a particular stack of these rods is 258 square units. Use one of the equations to find the number of rods in the stack. Check your answer by substituting the values for A and N into both equations.

3. In Problem 5.1, Brianna worked with rods that are 4 units long. To find the surface area of each stack, she slid the rods into a rectangular prism. She found the surface area of the prism and then added the extra area created by staggering the rods.

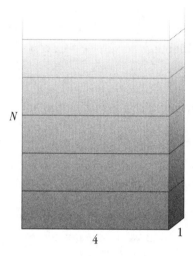

a. Write an expression for surface area that represents Brianna's method.

b. Show that your expression from part a is equivalent to the expressions in ACE question 2.

Connections

4. **a.** Write an equation for the surface area of a stack of N staggered rods if each rod is 12 units long.

b. If the surface area of a particular stack of these rods is 162 square units, how many rods are in the stack?

c. Write an equation for the volume of a stack of N of these rods.

Extensions

5. Consider rods of length 1, 2, 3, 4, 5, 6, 7, 8, 9, and 10 units.

    a. Make a table showing the surface area of a stack of N staggered rods of each length.

Length of rod	Surface area of a stack of N rods
1	
2	
3	

    b. Describe any patterns in your table.

    c. Write an equation for the surface area, A, of a stack of N rods of length L.

6. Rods of length 4 units are stacked to form a rectangular prism.

    a. What are the dimensions of the prism?

    b. Write an equation for the surface area, A, of the prism.

    c. What is the surface area of a prism 10 rods high and 10 rods wide?

    d. Is the relationship between the surface area and the number of rods linear, quadratic, exponential, or none of these? Explain your answer.

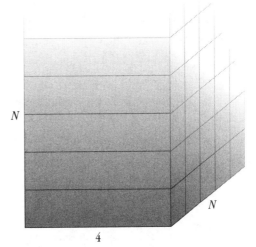

Mathematical Reflections

In this investigation, you wrote equations to represent the surface area of a stack of rods. You saw that different ways of thinking about the surface area led to different equations. These questions will help you summarize what you have learned:

1 **a.** Describe at least two of the strategies your class used to find the surface area of the stacks.

   b. Choose two of the strategies you described in part a, and show how they can be represented symbolically.

2 **a.** Describe situations that can be represented by several different, but equivalent, expressions. Explain how each expression represents a different way of thinking about the situation.

   b. For each situation you described in part a, use the distributive and commutative properties to show that the expressions are equivalent.

Think about your answers to these questions, discuss your ideas with other students and your teacher, and then write a summary of your findings in your journal.

Counting Cubes

Study the sequence of cube buildings below. What pattern do you see? Use the
pattern to build the next building in the sequence. Think about the steps you are
taking as you construct your building. The labels below the drawing illustrate one
way you might think about the pattern.

1 cube

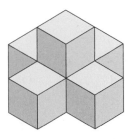

1 cube in the center and
5 arms with 1 cube each

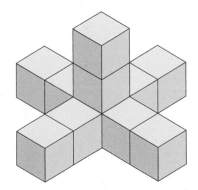

1 cube in the center and
5 arms with 2 cubes each

1. Describe a pattern *you* see in the cube buildings.

2. Use your pattern to write an expression for the number of cubes in the *n*th
building. You may find it helpful to make a table to organize your thinking.

3. Use your expression to find the number of cubes in the fifth building. Check
your result by constructing the fifth building and counting the cubes.

4. Look for a different pattern in the buildings. Describe the pattern, and use it to
write a different expression for the number of cubes in the *n*th building.

5. Start with one of the expressions you wrote, and use the distributive and commutative properties to write a third expression. Does the third expression suggest another pattern in the cube buildings? Explain.

6. Now make your own sequence of cube buildings by following a particular pattern.

 a. Sketch the first few buildings in your sequence, and write an expression for the number of cubes in the nth building.

 b. Challenge a classmate to describe the pattern in your buildings and to use the pattern to write an expression for the number of cubes in the nth building.

 c. Compare the expression you wrote in part a to the expression written by your classmate. If the expressions are not identical, use the commutative and distributive properties to prove or disprove their equivalence.

Looking Back and Looking Ahead

Unit Reflections

Working on the problems of this unit you learned and practiced the standard rules for using symbolic expressions in algebra. You learned the *order of operations* rules for evaluating expressions when you were given values of the variables involved. You found properties of numbers and operations that can be used to write algebraic expressions in *equivalent forms* and to *solve linear* and *quadratic equations* with algebraic reasoning.

Using Your Algebraic Reasoning—To test your understanding and skill in use of algebraic notation and reasoning, consider several problems that arise in the business of managing a summer concert tour for a popular music group.

1 *The promoter pays appearance fees to each group on the concert program. Some groups also get a share of the ticket sale income. Suppose that*

- *the lead group will be paid $15,000, plus $5 for every ticket sold.*
- *one of the other groups will receive $1500, plus $1.50 for every ticket sold.*
- *the third group will receive a flat fee of $1250.*

a. Write three different but equivalent equations showing how the promoter's expenses for performers, E, depend on the number of tickets sold for the concert, t.

  i. Write the first equation to show payments to each separate group.

  ii. Write the second equation to show the payment to the lead group and the combined payments to the other groups.

  iii. Write the third equation to show the simplest calculation of the total amount paid to the performers.

b. Suppose that tickets are priced at $25, $30, and $40.

  i. Write an equation that shows how the promoter's income from ticket sales, I, depends on the number sold of each type of ticket, x, y, and z.

  ii. Find the average income per ticket if there are sales of 5000 tickets at $25, 3000 tickets at $30, and 950 tickets sold at $40.

iii. Write an equation showing how the average income per ticket sold, V, depends on the variables x, y, z, and t.

2 *Suppose that the lead group has a new CD that will be sold only at concerts during the tour. Experience from other concert tours tells that the relation between the number of CDs sold, s, and price in dollars for the CD, p, can be modeled by the equation* $s = 10{,}000 - 200p$.

a. If the price is \$10, how many CDs will likely be sold?

b. What price(s) will yield sales of 3500 CDs?

c. What do the numbers 10,000 and -200 tell about the relation between CD price and the number that will be sold at a typical concert?

d. Write an equation expressing the income, I, from CD sales in terms of s and p. Then write another equation expressing I only in terms of p, the price of the CD.

e. What price(s) will yield total income of \$0?

f. What price(s) will yield maximum income?

3 *Suppose that concert seating is usually arranged in three sections as shown. Specific dimensions of the sections vary depending on the space available at each concert site.*

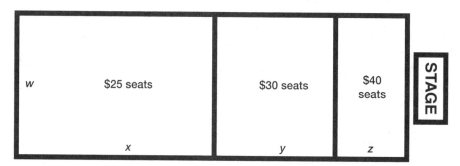

a. Write two equivalent equations showing the area of the entire seating area, A.

   i. In one equation, show how A depends on the areas of the three seating sections.

   ii. In the other equation, write an equivalent expression that requires fewer calculations to find A.

b. Seating is arranged to allow one square meter of space for every 2 people. Write two equivalent equations that show the number of seats, S, in terms of w, x, y, and z.

   i. In one equation, show how S depends on the numbers of seats in the separate sections.

   ii. In the other equation, write an expression that requires fewer calculations to find S.

c. When the concert is on a grassy field, aisles around and between the seating sections must be covered with boards that are 1.5 meters wide. How many square meters of board will be needed to cover the aisles for any given set of dimensions w, x, y, and z? Express your answer in at least two equivalent ways.

Explaining Your Reasoning—When you solve problems by writing and operating on symbolic expressions, you have to be careful to follow standard rules for use of such expressions and operations. When you present your conclusions to others, you should be able to explain your reasoning by application of those rules.

1. Evaluate the following expressions for the given values of x and y. Be prepared to explain the reasons for your answers.

   a. $5(x + 12y)$ when $x = {}^-7$ and $y = 0.5$

   b. $15 - 8x^2$ when $x = {}^-3$

   c. $\dfrac{5x^2 - 4x}{7 - 3x}$ when $x = {}^-2$

2. Write each of the following expressions in two different but equivalent forms. Be prepared to explain why the new forms are equivalent to those that are given.

   a. $7x(3 - 9x)$

   b. $15x + 8x^2$

   c. $(5x^2 - 9x + 7) + 4x(3 + 5x)$

   d. $(450 - 8a + 7b) - 3(5a - 2b)$

   e. $(2x + 3)(5x - 7)$

3. Solve the following equations by rewriting them in equivalent forms from which the roots are easy to find. Give the properties of numbers and operations that justify each step of your solution process.

   a. $9.5x + 12.5 = 50.5$ **b.** $3x^2 + 12x = 0$

   c. $(x + 4)(3x - 6) = 0$ **d.** $2(9x + 15) = 8 + 2x$

4. What does it mean to say that two algebraic expressions are *equivalent*?

The algebraic ideas and techniques you've used in this unit will be applied and extended in future mathematics courses and in science and business problems. The rules for expressing relationships among variables and for solving given equations are consistent around the world and in every discipline!

Glossary

commutative property of addition A mathematical property that states that the order in which quantities are added does not matter. For example, $5 + 7 = 7 + 5$ and $2x + 4 = 4 + 2x$. The commutative property of addition is sometimes called the *rearrangement property of addition*.

commutative property of multiplication A mathematical property that states that the order in which quantities are multiplied does not matter. For example, $5 \times 7 = 7 \times 5$ and $2x(4) = (4)2x$. The commutative property of multiplication is sometimes called the *rearrangement property of multiplication*.

distributive property A mathematical property used to rewrite expressions involving addition and multiplication. The distributive property states that for any three quantities a, b, and c, $a(b + c) = ab + ac$. If an expression is written as a factor multiplied by a sum, you can use the distributive property to *multiply* the factor by each term in the sum.

$$4(5 + x) = 4(5) + 4(x) = 20 + 4x$$

If an expression is written as a sum of terms and the terms have a common factor, you can use the distributive property to rewrite the expression as the common factor multiplied by a sum. This process is called *factoring*.

$$20 + 4x = 4(5) + 4(x) = 4(5 + x)$$

equivalent expressions Expressions that represent the same quantity. For example, $2 + 5$, $3 + 4$, and 7 are equivalent expressions. In this unit, you used the distributive and commutative properties to write equivalent expressions. For example, you can apply the distributive property to $2(x + 3)$ to write the equivalent expression $2x + 6$. By applying the commutative property to $2x + 6$, you can write the equivalent expression $6 + 2x$.

expanded form The form of an expression made up of sums or differences of terms rather than products of factors. The expressions $x^2 + 7x + 12$ and $x^2 + 2x$ are in expanded form.

factored form The form of an expression made up of products of factors rather than sums or differences of terms. The expressions $(x + 3)(x + 4)$ and $x(x - 2)$ are in factored form.

parabola The graph of a quadratic function. A parabola has a line of symmetry that passes through the maximum point if the graph opens downward or through the minimum point if the graph opens upward.

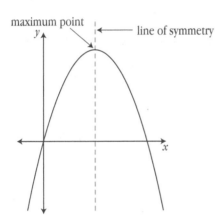 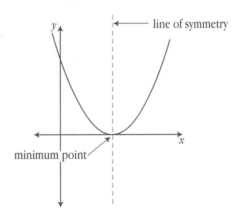

roots The roots of an equation are the values of x that make y equal 0. For example, the roots of $y = x^2 + 5x$ are $^-5$ and 0 because $(^-5)^2 + 5(^-5) = 0$ and $0^2 + 5(0) = 0$. The roots of $y = x^2 + 5x$ are the solutions to the equation $0 = x^2 + 5x$. The roots of an equation are the x-intercepts of its graph.

term An expression with numbers and/or variables multiplied together. In the expression $3x^2 - 2x + 10$, $3x^2$, ^-2x, and 10 are terms.

Glosario

expresiones equivalentes Expresiones que representan la misma cantidad, como por ejemplo $2 + 5$, $3 + 4$ y 7. En esta unidad, usaste las propiedades distributiva y conmutativa para escribir expresiones equivalentes. Por ejemplo, puedes aplicar la propiedad distributiva a $2(x + 3)$ para escribir la expresión equivalente $2x + 6$. Mediante la aplicación de la propiedad conmutativa a $2x + 6$, puedes escribir la expresión equivalente $6 + 2x$.

forma de factores La forma de una expresión compuesta de productos de factores en vez de sumas o diferencias de términos. Las expresiones $(x + 3)(x + 4)$ y $x(x - 2)$ están representadas en forma de factores.

forma desarrollada La forma de una expresión compuesta de sumas o diferencias de términos en vez de productos de factores. Las expresiones $x^2 + 7x + 12$ y $x^2 + 2x$ están representadas en forma desarrollada.

parábola La gráfica de una función cuadrática. Una parábola tiene un eje de simetría que pasa por el punto máximo si la gráfica se abre hacia abajo o por el punto mínimo si la gráfica se abre hacia arriba.

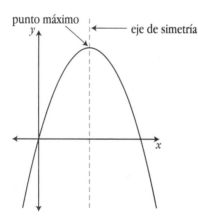

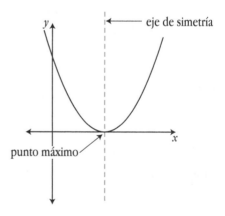

propiedad conmutativa de la multiplicación Una propiedad matemática que dice que el orden en que se multiplican los factores no tiene importancia. Por ejemplo, $5 \times 7 = 7 \times 5$ y $2x(4) = (4)2x$. A veces se la llama *propiedad de reordenamiento de la multiplicación*.

propiedad conmutativa de la suma Una propiedad matemática que dice que el orden en que se suman las cantidades no tiene importancia. Por ejemplo, $5 + 7 = 7 + 5$ y $2x + 4 = 4 + 2x$. A veces se la llama *propiedad de reordenamiento de la suma*.

propiedad distributiva Una propiedad matemática usada para reescribir expresiones que incluyen la suma y la multiplicación. La propiedad distributiva se establece para tres cantidades cualesquiera a, b y c, $a(b + c) = ab + ac$. Si una expresión se escribe como la multiplicación de un factor por una suma, la propiedad distributiva puede usarse para *multiplicar* el factor por cada término de la suma.

$$4(5 + x) = 4(5) + 4(x) = 20 + 4x$$

Si una expresión se escribe como la suma de los términos y los términos tienen un factor común, la propiedad distributiva puede usarse para reescribir o descomponer en factores la expresión como la multiplicación del factor común por una suma.

$$20 + 4x = 4(5) + 4(x) = 4(5 + x)$$

raíces Las raíces de una ecuación son los valores de x que hacen que y equivalga a 0. Por ejemplo, las raíces de $y = x^2 + 5x$ son $^-5$ y 0 porque $(^-5)^2 + 5(^-5) = 0$ y $0^2 + 5(0) = 0$. Las raíces de $y = x^2 + 5x$ son las soluciones de la ecuación $0 = x^2 + 5x$. Las raíces de una ecuación son los puntos de intersección del eje de las x de la gráfica de esa ecuación.

término Una expresión con números y/o variables multiplicados entre sí. En la expresión $3x^2 - 2x + 10$, $3x^2$, ^-2x y 10 son términos.

Index